With Midnight Down Your Throat

With Midnight Down Your Throat

Poems by

Caitlyn Curran

Willow Springs Books
Spokane, Washington

With Midnight Down Your Throat is the debut collection in the Emma Howell Rising Poets series.

No part of this book may be reproduced or transmitted in any form or by any means, electronic or mechanical, including photocopy, recording, or any information storage and retrieval system now known to to be invented, without permission in writing from the publisher, except by a reviewer who wishes to quote brief passages in connection with a review written for inclusion in a magazine, newspaper, or broadcast.

Cataloging and Publication Information available from the Library of Congress upon request.

Cover Artwork: Connor "Phib" Dainty
Cover Design: Rin Baatz
Interior Design: Rin Baatz, Alexandria Ross, Megan Robinson

FIRST EDITION

Willow Springs Books, Spokane, WA 99202
Copyright © 2022 Caitlyn Curran
Printed in the United States of America
All Rights Reserved
Printed by Gray Dog Press
ISBN: 978-1-955082-03-7

This and other Willow Springs Books publications may be viewed online at willowspringsbooks.org.

—For Lester Lara

CONTENTS

Foreword	
Duck Duck Goose	1
Pretty White Trash Ghazal	2
Self-Portrait as the Thomas Fire with Displaced Laugh Track	3
A Bumper Sticker Tells Me What Belongs	4
Sapphic for Asking My Brother about His Medications	5
Horror Vacui	6
Paso Robles Sestina	7
All I Wanted	9
Email from My Mother with Subject Line: Gun-isms	10
With Midnight Down Your Throat You Try to Sing:	11
How to Lose Your God	12
The Interesting Stuff Lives in Holes	13
Holding On	14
Elegy Stitched Together	15
Another Litany for Corpses	16
Sisters	17
Last Summer	18
Tracing	19
Fish Tank	20
And He Shall Be Called	21
Bones	22
The Babysitter	23
Daddy	24
Evacuation	25
The Danners	26
Talking to the Goat	31

I Am Not Your Aunt	32
Thetys Vagina	33
Color	34
My Sister Was a Fish, and Air	35
The Land of Ordinary Violence	36
Sister in Recovery	44
Let's Not Say	46
One Day, When	47
When My Last Boyfriend Wrapped His Truck Around a Tree	48
Becoming With	49
Growing Up Is the Most Luxurious Thing I've Ever Let Happen	50
Painting My House Vantablack	51

Foreword

Once, daring light... That's the phrasal synthesis that opens and closes this powerful debut by Caitlyn Curran. And it resonates with the book's precise instincts for timing and risk—how working to reconcile a personal and familial legacy that intersects with collective experiences of poverty, mental illness, addiction, domestic violence, gun violence, sexual abuse, infertility, sudden deaths, &c. (any one of which, without proper support, could produce a darkness thick enough to diminish one's voice) can sometimes feel like challenging a vast and impartial history of stars to urgently answer your individual trauma. But *With Midnight Down Your Throat* goes there, and bless it for doing so, because Curran delivers us to the other side of profound grief while tracking remarkable faith and restoring the sacredness of possibility. In fact, the book's own literacy of reflection and irreverence invites me to consider a syntactical variation to that phrasal orientation: *Once daring, light*. And it's this kind of conversion through difficult wonder that I feel driving much of this book's poetic reckoning with lived experience.

Echoed some by the formal variety found throughout—while mostly in free-verse, this book also trades in the ghazal, sapphic verse, the sestina, the sonnet—I also want to celebrate how Curran's poems feel more concerned with the integrity of re-vision than with the fragility of proof. This comes through strongly in the poems that display earlier models of the speaker's working consideration.

> I thought if I asked for so little, I'd never be full
> but I'd never starve. I walk around the house
> without a shadow, like a flame.
> 			("Evacuation")

As Curran demonstrates, recovery depends on contending with what's general and specific and unfinished about our realities of loss, often alongside a mythic-like patience:

> And whatever is left behind in the breaking
> builds another type of door
> in my body. Where I knock
> and knock and wait.
> ("The Interesting Stuff Lives in Holes")

But the hard work of such waiting doesn't necessitate an avoidance of pleasure. At times, Curran uses humor with stunning effect in this book, brilliantly plucking at the formal and tonal attentions that run between tragedy and comedy, her bluesy contribution to the reparative recognition that grief and joy can (or must) share human chords. Perhaps no sadness could rupture this, but a healing might ride this scale home.

I've needed books like this my whole life, books that map with intention and integrity the valleys of a life's sorrows. Not to deepen the reach of grief (grief needs no such extension; as we know, it can go on forever) but, through poetry's imagery and music and alterity, to staunch the ability for memory or despair to place us even one psychic inch lower inside the land of our losses, which would only make our ascent to safety seem less possible. No, this book bides for her and us alike. Here's Curran again, in the poem "Growing Up Is the Most Luxurious Thing I've Ever Let Happen," which appears near the end of this collection:

> Yes, I still hear something sinister
> in the quiet moments, like I did as a child,
> tying my shoelaces in the mornings after
> the loud nights. These days, I've started to enjoy
> the sound of my own name in different frequencies.
> Which is to say, I'm handing out forgiveness
> like raffle tickets, like tiny moons, like costume
> jewelry, like cold water from the hose.

And Curran concludes the poem:

everything is fine. Still, I walk the dog
in the evening—her breath, small clouds,
and I look into the warmlit windows
of every beautiful home, their ordinary paintings
in frames over clean walls, and I want to get so small
I can crawl into their mailbox, wait
for a kind hand to bring me inside.

    I'm already in awe of what Caitlyn Curran has come to offer, and I trust that I'm only among the first wave of converts. What an honor and profound sense of luck to find myself in the position to say *yes* to this tremendous first book. Now let me get out of its damn way…

    —Geffrey Davis

DUCK DUCK GOOSE

Once, Mom got us out. Packed my sister
and me into the wood-paneled van.
Middle of the night, maybe summer.

All in our pajamas at the park. I remember
the gazebo lit up from the middle, though I still can't
make out Mom's face, or my sister's

gapped teeth. How memory can shape itself into history:

middle of the night, maybe summer.

The gazebo lit up. But the gazebo never
had any lights. Still, I hold this memory like a map:
once, Mom got us out. Me and my sister.

We played until morning. I imagine I fell asleep in the car,
and Mom carried me inside, but this wasn't how it happened:

middle of the night   maybe summer

escape route   wet grass.

It never happened at all—the gazebo never
had any lights. This memory is a map,
and no one else remembers. Look: once Mom got us out.

PRETTY WHITE TRASH GHAZAL

When friends first start to come over in elementary school they look
around, say *Huh, I thought you were rich.* But no, we're pretty white trash.

I don't know it then, I just know that their house smells great, has a pool,
& that teachers look at me like they're worried (like I'm pretty white trash).

Eventually, friends aren't allowed over anyway. Brother wears a wallet chain & too-
big leather jacket. Sister smokes pills off tinfoil in the kitchen. Pretty white trash,

we hungry kids, & we grow to know it. Hanging too late in the park, eating the cool
nights, searching for half-smoked butts. Hey-mistering forties, you know, pretty white trash

stuff. Dad gets his throat slit open by his own sister, his blood spools
out: Popov vodka & meth. Pretty standard, I think. I'm pretty white trash

for laughing about it. He survives, holds his stitches together, stays cool.
He winks when he says *Shaving accident.* See, it's all good in Pretty-White-Trash

Town where my sister breaks Dad's nose outside of Big Bad Bubba's Bad-to-the-Bone BBQ.
It's dollar-shots night after the fair. A Bic lighter as a fist pack protects her pretty, white trash

hand from breaking. Dad's so proud he flickers, says *Caitlyn, your sister's got a mean right hook.*

SELF-PORTRAIT AS THE THOMAS FIRE WITH DISPLACED LAUGH TRACK

I wake with my mother in her bed,
she's already smoking and watching the news.
The Thomas Fire undresses mountains
to the south. California closes its eyes
in a bowl of smoke. I light a cigarette and Mom
moves the ashtray between us on the bed.
In the other room, a laugh track—
my brother watching TV. Every fifteen seconds *Hahaha*
like a flock of ordinary birds. How
do we account for loss, in vegetation or ash?
The body count: two. The dog on the news runs away
and comes back to the razed foundation of her home.
Strong winds are forecast again for Wednesday—*Hahaha...*
I've laughed into the fire winds too,
made light of my charred parts: whole
lives carved out by the white crack of heat. I hold
my tongue to the ash, here I am
asking for nothing but what flame can give.

A BUMPER STICKER TELLS ME WHAT BELONGS

In this parking lot of discarded snow,
the Toyota Corolla, saint of the A to B,

proclaimer of *I-think-I-cans* up the scattershot
hills and past the old barns, baroque

in their leanings and rot—I imagine
this unremarkable engine, four stroke

and tired of its long life, wears this badge
all through town, the sticker that says

I support arming babies in the womb!
and boasts a fetus sucking its thumb

and holding an AK-47
(but Kalashnikov's amniotic fluid tasted

like his mother's dinner:
baked chicken, garlic bread, and ripe

tomatoes. It didn't taste like metal
or blood, it didn't feel like trigger

or hairpin or automatic). You want
a birth so bad you'd open me with steel

and replace me with bullet shell.
My body is already a weapon

the way I explode and divide,
the way I know what will exist

in me: blood, egg, magma, a sickloud laughter
that could empty this town.

SAPPHIC FOR ASKING MY BROTHER ABOUT HIS MEDICATIONS

—For Criste

Transmissions misfire in channels and you
set the volume, come to the table, don't eat.
Easy isn't possible. I know, brother,
growing up crooked.

Tired hands, trailer parks in the cow-cry night—you
sleep it off for weeks and you haven't even
left the house except to the neighbors' for a
haircut and a fifth

of burning, knock-off peppermint schnapps that has you
handcuffed later on their lawn, hospital bound—
either there or jail. And how many pills for
sleep? The white caps will

twist and lock. You mumble in the cherry light of
blankets over lamps and windows. Standing
here: our shared and hapless blood in a too-still
hallway—flags fall limp.

HORROR VACUI

With centuries of cardinals hammering the sky. A kiln of startled feathers make a carnal and clayfire mess. The blue shadow of the ones who disappear. This is why I cry *don't leave stay for one more* while I kick the chair out from under you. You are anyone. Standing in the shedding possibility of my body. Or maybe loss is specific. The stained glass of my sternum and this parade of occult data. What glue, what birdshit, what pinch, what heat holds these pieces together? I populate my apartment with my own breath until I can float in it and the plants die. A field is never empty, it is noisy with field.

PASO ROBLES SESTINA

By fourteen, I was always walking out
the door late, Mom calling after *Where
are you going? Riding in cars with boys?*—*Yes,
Ma.* Driving the dark roads toward night,
sleeping on Ronnie's basement floor
drunk, and skipping first period again.

I get out of Saturday school (again and again).
Mom doesn't worry, says worry's a sin. So I'm out
in the riverbank, toes sunk in the cold sand floor.
The cops come and we hide in the bushes (where
Lester and I first held hands). That night
they pour out every beer and let us go. Yes,

they let us all drive home. (We had *Yes*
etched in our throats, a chant against
the lull of every dead stoplight.)
Stealing beer from the ampm, kissing Lester out
front of the trashed Motel 6 room where
someone breaks the mirror, leaves blood on the floor.

There's a hole in every door
at home (and most walls, too). Yes,
it's easy to walk out and go, but where?
So Erin and I shoplift from Walmart again:
backpacks full. It's not an in-and-out
job. We can stay here all night.

Jordan's out on bail, goes back next week, so tonight
I have most of his stash bagged up on the floor
of my Civic, stuffed in a Colgate box. I run out
quick. In the Albertsons parking lot, his eyes
light up when I hand him the cash, so I re-up again.
He's got money now for his books in County (where

he'll be for a few years). Same parking lot where
a stranger buys us a handle of vodka (that night
Lester dies over and over again
in that truck he's in). Always, it floors
and flips four times. I don't close my eyes.
Every time, I run and find him thrown out,

lying between the tire and the quiet root floor
below the oak   (and I do understand this wasn't a way to live, yes—)
when all sound drains out.

ALL I WANTED

I wanted Skittles when he died
and Marlboros—
so whenever someone asked *Can I bring you anything?*
that's what I said.

    Sour Skittles, their grainy choke
    to make your eyes well up. I'd suck them bald
    and sweet, then swallow. Marlboro 27s.
    My touch stayed sour.
    My raw tongue a thin machine of *Thank-yous.*

That night of the wreck
I couldn't find a lighter.
      Kept pleading with the cops—*Matches? Anything?*
      There's got to be a fire somewhere I can lift
      my mouth to.

    After, I wouldn't eat for months without choking.
    Spitting out my food like I never was
    programmed to swallow.

Now, these years pile up and I eat them with salt.
Like a freckle or a splinter,
each mundane hour becomes a part
of me without my permission,

      as he was, with the tire on his back, part truck.

EMAIL FROM MY MOTHER WITH SUBJECT LINE: GUN-ISMS

She shuffles her feet on the concrete
of memory—I can always tell it's her
outside, shaking snake oil on the grass.
Gun-ism: *Because I can't throw a rock 1,155 feet per second.*
O rock, stay where you are. We don't need you anymore.
I've only seen my mother cry twice. One night
my brother got dangerous, she loaded us in the van,
threw all the guns in the back. In the ampm parking lot
we waited it out. My brother said
I'll take out as many motherfuckers as I can
with me. Might as well.
He walks softly today, stirs up static
on the carpet of Mom's trailer. Sleeps
into the corners of his room. Gun-ism:
Now I lay me down to sleep, beside my bed
a Glock I keep. If you let me, Mother,
I'd cry too. Last week, I tried.
The space around my body is too loud.
I'll dig my hands into the ammunition, find
every moment hollowed by its own disaster.

WITH MIDNIGHT DOWN YOUR THROAT YOU TRY TO SING:

to the shaking dog in your closet
to the missing headstone
to the blank page of winter
to your father stepping into the grave
to the back row at church
to the bay horse with his ears back
to the morning when it comes
to your sister methadone-sleeping in the afternoon,
       pants unbuttoned
to your mother rolling cigarettes in the quiet trailer park
to the relentless stampede of joy
to your sister graduating college
to your brother blasting Insane Clown Posse in the parking lot
       of your elementary school
to the Mentos in the Sam's Choice Cola
to explosions and the recoil
to the smoke and what's left
toward the note you won't reach
to the greening night
to the seam of your father's throat
to the laugh you allow yourself
to your brother living past now
to yourself as a child
to yourself, hiding in the closet
to yourself, shaking with the dog.

HOW TO LOSE YOUR GOD

You can follow Jesus around town
as a young girl—each day lifting
your hands higher in worship, head lower
in prayer. Singing hymns
in a bright falsetto, so people
in the rows ahead turn around
and smile. If your knees
know the carpet of sanctuary
before they know blood, it is likely
you will baptize your Barbies
in any worthy body of water. Know,
still, a pastor's teenage son can ask to play,
then open your favorite sunflower dress.
Try counting the disciples in your head.
Eat of His body with a newer hunger—
the wafer sour on your tongue.
If you decide you don't know how
to be saved, consider the unknowing enough.
In the gaps and fits of your body, you'll still
find prayer. Sometimes you'll look
and you just won't believe
that you're still there.

THE INTERESTING STUFF LIVES IN HOLES

in my brain, I joke, trying to count

the number of times I've boiled myself

on ecstasy—a wet firefly surging

between the teeth of a dog.

Why not drive the eyes back

into the old cupboard of the skull in search

of sweat and clench and burn?

I know holes so well I forget

the story behind each one

in the walls and doors

of the house I grew up in.

The tape and spackle littered

like small mounds of dirt.

And whatever is left behind in the breaking

builds another type of door

in my body. Where I knock

and knock and wait.

HOLDING ON

He fell asleep with his fingers pinching
my armpit hair, just tight enough
so I couldn't slip away—how he holds
a cherry tomato, slices
it down the middle, wetness
spilling over the blade onto the cutting
board as the two halves cling to each other
before rocking back, apart—and I rooted myself
there in the sweetness of it, my hair
in his fingers, thinking about how, recently,
enormous swells rocked the Oregon coast,
and a man took his two young children
to watch the water rise like a roar
in the throat. When they got too close,
the ocean took the children in,
made them water, too. When they lost
their feet underneath them, how easy
it must have been to move like water,
too slippery to hold. How quickly they unlearned
to breathe. Then: just a man
on the shore, his two empty hands.

ELEGY STITCHED TOGETHER

It's just like you've lost your keys
for good and no spare, but no, really, you've lost
your car or you've forgotten where you live,
the street and color of joy. Is your hair falling out? It is now
in strands like ridiculous eels at the surface of the brown river.
Slitting up and back down with their slender tailbodies, rinsing down
the drain. Remember I would straighten out your black hair
with my fingers—it was always on end and nothing like mine.
It just wouldn't sit. It's just that you sat in the truck,
but I remember you underneath with the tire on your back.
No one would help me lift it.
A tire seems necessary like employment or a trustworthy dentist
but it will burn and spin and land like split-open
fireworks unable to stop exploding in a young hand.
It's just that there is more than one fuse. The hand is gone
but someone picks it back up in the gravel.
The show explodes back into the dark sky.
It's just that I saw your blood underneath
my fingernails and kept it there for weeks.
I never wanted it to wash away like common dirt.
After each shower I would check and make sure
it was still there, and it was. Now I try to bite it away
with loose-teeth dreams in the mirror they are falling to dust
like unstable bricks, like a dog her jaw shifted from the car
that hit her, her last face a growl her shining long bite-me teeth
dry and misplaced, but the blood stays there. Doesn't it?

ANOTHER LITANY FOR CORPSES

and for the living
                        and for those
in urns and for the smacking of dust
in dry teeth
            and you don't need
teeth anymore and when you did
you loved mangoes and mangoes
keep slipping out of their blooms
small fresh lungs
                       and there's you
underground clicking the thin olive tree
and the horse kicking at the wind
or you
        in all cremation fire and for what
used to breathe and for breathing
gas giants of what dies too
and lonely in their color
against the black

        and for the wetlands
of a kind and stupid promise we might dream up
and for you corpses and for you rot I have nothing

        and for your funeral
clothes and for the need
for dress and flowers and for casket-shine
in dirt in ash and for what

SISTERS

We couldn't stand
to be inside with the heat
and the glare, making everything
dark—the sun blindness that stayed
for years. We'd move our nakedness
to the lawn or the broken spa,
chemical-flaked and filled
with hose water. The hose water
spat back nothing
but more glare.
For a week in July, we moved our nakedness
to France, living off savings
from selling pills, to smoke on balconies
over the busy rue. We'd take
our glare with us—
that heat and dark. We knew
we were the same, our bodies
crafted in memory
and severe witness.
Bare-breasted above,
we knew no one
would look up.

LAST SUMMER

I left that man alone
with his green eyes.
My loneliness is hungrier
than noise. Sucking at the air.
By gasfire he'd hold me and we'd grow
into our pupils eventually. Baggies
of coke eating through
another night.
Here's what I know:

I feed off myself. I'm so afraid
of being eaten, I pick away
my own edges. This leaving,
this leaving. Watch me
spin the air between
us into bone.

TRACING

I draw a wildfire. Is it still

                a wildfire

                if I start it? Look

into the edge blur

and light. Wash your hands with the heat.

                Erase fire. What's left:

my sister. She isn't her flames

                anymore.

Is she still my sister when she dies

in a dream?   Look at the memory of fire:

drawing itself as subtraction.

                The body of flame

in touch   and collision.

Meanwhile, her fingers slouch

against my face,   trace more deft lines.

FISH TANK

      There's always been a bullet hole
in the living room window.
         Engines of flies gather in fists.
    Dad shatters the fish tank,
       stumbles to bed.
               Dad sets up cans in the yard—
                  bright lures. We sit in the empty
   spa like a trench,
old BB gun against my shoulder.
             I'm a good shot.
I ask for a .22 for Christmas. I'm seven.
        He laughs, proud, when he sees it on the list.
    I know water
        spreads like a web. My toes prune,
picking the fish up.
I'm not angry.   I didn't get the gun.
      There's always been a bullet hole.
It spiders out in tics. Flies find their way in.
    Glass is not like water. It cracks or it doesn't. I pick
the fish up. They flutter in bowls
              until morning.

AND HE SHALL BE CALLED

My mother taped it on her door (the list
of all Christ's names) a poster just in case
we kids forgot. In one he's called   *the Rose
of Sharon—*   her name, proof of her witness.

A glossy poster with edges burnt to ash
          (or so it's made to look: old scroll of faith).
     It reads: *Messiah,*   *Shiloh,*   *Prince of Peace,*
The Door.   Fitting, I know. Taped there in place

          and covering a nasty, jagged hole.
So that we might forget   *Man of Sorrows*
     Judge   she locked herself in   *Bishop of Souls*
so that the door bore the brunt of all the blows.

She patched it up and prayed again, in hopes
of more than shadow from the holy ghost.

BONES

When my father lived
in California, I'd drive up
to visit him. I couldn't go
inside, so we'd sit on the porch,
drink beer, watch the goat
scatter droppings. Everything
that wasn't said, bones kept
in a pocket of thought. I still can't open
my jaw enough to speak.

See how the bones map the face
of these hills, determine the dry grass,
the way it burns. A cracked valley
clavicle. Pelvic pond: dry. See how a grave
becomes two sprigs of willow
a child brings to their wet mouth.

THE BABYSITTER

Here, I'm two. The shag carpet
kicks up static in lamplight,
and she pets me as sparks set
off of her long fingernails. I eat
from a bowl of cold chopped
hot dogs. She's teaching me
to read and write, so I'm tracing sloppy
letters, spelling *Jesus* and *baby*
in a workbook. Yes, my sister
is here, too. She'll spend three years
in another room with the babysitter's
youngest son, thinking she'll get out of there,
soon,
                soon,   *soon.*

DADDY

      tell me about your day.   I'd like to thank you
            for my spidersoft hair,   my secondhand

boozing blonde.   Family is the backbone
     of society, a father
  told me once.   My backbone
    hurts,   Daddy.   This society squeals
        against   my shoulders, zips me down
to coccyx. I don't have to shave
         my legs anymore, Daddy. No one makes me
  food, it costs   money so I don't
     eat much   these days.   You made me eat
    those peppers   and the dog
laughed at you from under the porch.   The dog that crushed her own
   puppies.   Daddy you're sobbing on the phone on my thirteenth birthday
again today.   No one can be angry with you.
    You were so good at talking down
  the police when they came.   You charm,   I'll hang
    you from the rearview.   Your cut facets throw sparks.
     Someday I'll learn each edge.

    Today, come closer. I'll unlace your boots.

EVACUATION

The night we talk about breaking up, I walk
around the house with a camera, naming
all of our valuables for insurance: here's our TV,
here's our red couch, our fiddle-leaf fig. There is a fire
coming closer, smoke so low and thick we can't see
our neighbors' homes. How dare a fire ask
for so much without a lick of shame? His bike,
my birdfeeder, our little fishing boat. For a moment,
for a week, I think that flames may as well eat
our home if we can't learn to live
in it together. Smoke hangs in the living
room like old party streamers. The plants choke
and curl inward. Ten dead, zero percent contained.
I thought if I asked for so little, I'd never be full
but I'd never starve. I walk around the house
without a shadow, like a flame.

THE DANNERS

I.

Jerica accused you
of kissing Johnny, so you
punched her in the face.
She screamed for her daddy
as blood smeared her upper
lip. You thought of it
later, kissing Johnny, swimming
whirlpools in the steel stock
tank pool, because his fingertips
sometimes grazed your ankles
and you'd never kissed
a boy but, no, you hadn't
forgiven him for throwing
that Chihuahua
you found in the field—
you could still hear
his laugh, and right
then you wished
you could punch Johnny
in his crossed-over
teeth, but he was too big
so you swam
faster.

II.

You left Jerica's baby
shower early, too stoned,
and you forgot to bring a gift
anyway. You just showed
to see her swelled up
like that, because you can
only remember her scrawny
and tan, the mole on her upper lip
with the blood running down,
how she smelled
sleepovers
touching herself over cotton
panties, showing you,
and that breathiness a haze
around her like an aura.
Chris, her mom,
tells you not to be a stranger,
but you have been
for years now.

III.

Johnny and Jerica pulled whiskey
from a Coke can at their father's
wake. Half-drunk, cranking a wrench
on the old lawn mower,
John's heart burst. His favorite
song played: *Down
in the west Texas town of El Paso.*
Your father choked on song.
Johnny and his buddies kicked
at trash collecting
by the old swing.

IV.

The electricity was out
on 700 Klau Mine Rd.
In the darkness,
the stench
of the rattler farm climbed
up the wall where the cages
were stacked. In a meth
haze they'd hear
the hissing songs
and dance to the rattles
like twitching cats.
Three a.m. Johnny stared
into the fire, burning trash,
then rushed for his .45 when he heard
his mother scream. He shot her
boyfriend nine times, all over.
The police found the man
lying naked
in a doorway. Johnny bit
down with his crossed-over
teeth on forty years
and swallowed.

V.

Jerica and I thought he'd run away—
a stray in the high dead
grass—but instead he ran right
up and licked our faces.
An hour passed, we tried
sit, lie down, shake, named
him Frankie. We were
happy to show him off
when Johnny walked up.
I know another trick he can do.
Look, he can fly.
So Johnny scooped up the dog
and chucked him high
as he could with his new boyish
strength, laughing. And still
laughing when Frankie landed
with a squeal on a broken
leg. We girls ran to John
who got his gun
when he saw the dog
had no collar. *Another trick...*
the shot echoed off
the trees in the gully.

TALKING TO THE GOAT

—For Joseph Fahey

I named you after a boy I knew.
The first in my life to die. He did,
in his bed. But you are a goat
with landscapes of mountains

in your strange eyes. All through the first
night you bleated alone until your small
voice left. But it grew back—
sharp rattles in the field.

I know it is unusual for goats
to have a middle name.
When we walk, you climb
right up the old olive tree

to look down on me
and bleat in your rhythm
like a laugh. The branches are yours,
now just out of reach.

I AM NOT YOUR AUNT

I was almost an aunt three times—
there were two spasms of blood, even once

a baby, born screeching like a gull.
The first must have slipped

in the dark when the sky unbuttoned
and swayed in moans. The second,

a tucked seed hiding its face in the open
pomegranate, its cracked peel.

The second slipped too, or scraped
through rough swells. And the third,

we know about you. My near-nephew,
my brother is not your father.

Sing for it. Open your dark wet throat
and howl. You will not know us.

THETYS VAGINA

You deep ocean salp, I have more
questions for you. Do you foam
at the touch, melt like lard
in the window of the sun?
I would dig my hands
inside, scoop out your light
to spread across my face.
Glow through in your jelly
afterbirth. What is your citrus
taste, your formless bright?
You join yourself with yourself—
a chain, a clone, a twelve-inch maw
to open and eat the smallest
of what floats in the dense waters.
Your nerves are like mine, developing
cords and pools in my mother's womb.
We are sisters of the embryo,
until I become backbone
and you become male,
female, male, female.
You stay hidden from the sun
so I only find you here, dead
on shore. Of course.
How could you last
with all your shining
down so very deep?

COLOR

The child thinks of coins
when looking at her grandmother's thin wrists.

This must be how to move in shadow, the child thinks.

The grandmother is blind and maybe
she has seen a stone fence
stacked in mud among sheep.
Maybe, as a child.

Her name tumbles in time to another country
called Ohio. She does her makeup
perfectly every secret
morning by touch.

The child scuffs across the carpet,
sits on the bed.
She grabs the child's dress, holds
it close to her face, asks
Is this orange? Yes.

Orange has always looked so good on you.

MY SISTER WAS A FISH, AND AIR

could not sustain her. She was caught
up out of the world for a moment, seized

algaeic on the line, thin and blue,
spitting up foam—gasping

more water, more morphine, crushed
Oxy on wrinkled tinfoil. A punch

to the chest brought her back,
tossed her into the warm polymer water

she breathed in through a straw or hollowed
pen. The surface of the water, fissures

hardening with chill. She thought of this
as just another hook in her cheek,

a small scar. This can happen
after so much swimming.

THE LAND OF ORDINARY VIOLENCE

*

Here, I can forget the name
of my first love's mother
for an entire week. The woman
who brought him to America
after his father died at twenty-eight, who lost
her only child when he was nineteen. Suddenly,
frying an egg in the afternoon, her name
smacks me like a dark wind
and, from then on, *Tess* is all I can hear
in the rusty mouth of the mailbox,
in the shudder of keys in my pocket.
I sing *Tess* to myself absentmindedly
as if it were an old hit. She's everything
I know about the wicked
occupation of living.

*

Here, a bad dog is the object
of my wildest affection.
And every bite she gives—
a boy's leg, a woman's face,
the neighbor's cat's newly punctured
lung—becomes a new freckle
that I stare at in the mirror.
The more I look, the more genuinely
I love it. Because every hole
is also mine, every grief a meal.

*
Here, Dad shows up drunk
to the funeral and, parking, hits Tess's
car. *I just bumped it*. He snivels
into my shoulder. Later, loses
his keys in the pews. Tess says she wanted
an open casket but *His face,* she says,
Did you see his face? I didn't.
She holds her hands to her forehead.
I just saw his back and his black
mess of hair. Put my fingers through it.
Came away with blood.

*

Here, Elliot Rodger lives down the street.
It's late May. We leave the restaurant,
go to Christian's house to play guitar and sing.
One more song, let's stay for one more song,
and we do. Now our friends are under
the restaurant tables, the glass storefront, gone.
Walking home, Molly and I see the parade
of red and blue lights, the sirens
like broken chords. To our right,
someone calling out *I've been shot in the leg*.

*

Here, a crowd forms outside
the movie theater. A woman's hair
tangles into my sister's fists
as she brings the woman's face
to her knee again and again.
Because I talked during the movie
and the woman shushed me.
Weeks before, our father grabbed
my sister's hair like this, slammed
her forehead into the wall. In the car,
my sister shakes, keys in hand, repeating
What happened? What just happened?

*

Here, half of my molar falls
away while eating popcorn
and I only notice after,
searching for stray kernels
between my teeth. The flesh
there: soft, unhiding, dark.
It is months before I can
get it patched, so I spend
my days probing the hole,
tonguing the wreck of sharp edges.

*

Here, my mother stops
my sister from slamming
the glass ashtray into the base
of my father's skull. *The medulla
oblongata* my mother says, recalling
that night: my brother cowered
in the corner as our father's
body raged in a blur above.
He wouldn't have noticed my sister
behind him. The ashtray so heavy
in the possibility of her small hands.

*

Here, mailboxes no longer torment
me. The night of the crash, before
we all stepped into separate cars, the driver
stumbles, drops his keys. Now
I'm nervous—insisting everyone go
slow. The truck behind (the one *he's* in
with his clean face and warm, brown
arms) passes on the left, clips the mailbox,
flips. Everyone survives but him. Before
I find his body, I am sure that everybody
is fine. Because everyone I love
is still so much alive.

SISTER IN RECOVERY

    —For Sissy

As we drive to the clinic
her rage is a heavy stone,
shining and valuable.
She changes the lyrics of the country
songs on the radio into something
about chopping her ex's balls off.
We always arrive only just in time,
the methadone waiting thick and green
in its quiet brown bottles.
This drab building looks
almost warm, a chapel
of coming-and-going devotions
to this tedious god. Each dose
a heavy pane of stained glass
depicting a sleeping woman.
And she sleeps like this for five years
on the old blue couch, holes deep
in the upholstery from letting the pet
rats root around and nest.
When Mom gets home, my sister wakes,
slams doors, screams
I told you and you did nothing. I was a child.
Because nothing ever happened
to my body there, at the babysitter's
house, the one with three sons.
Because my sister lay down
instead. Now, we drive
to the clinic, smoke weed,
watch TV. With her help, I haven't been
to the seventh grade in a month.
I have my first bout of acne,

my face unfamiliar and ballooned,
so I stay home and we delete the messages
from the school coming through
on the answering machine.
She makes me veggie scrambles,
steams a washcloth
with tea tree oil. With both hands,
she holds it to my cheeks
and closes her eyes.

LET'S NOT SAY

The swing out by the tack shed has been re-roped
        in hot August memory.
My voice is already my mother's, pressed
        by riverstones, grit, burn.
Together, we drag damp hay bales around the fire
        of my sister's broken heart.
We stand on the same side of a memory,
        itching to be clean.
Jaws click in the corners of the house. We pick
        hay from our clothes.
There are nests of tall shadows in the long grass.
We pick hay from our clothes for generations.
        With the same small hands.

ONE DAY, WHEN

certain things just stopped being
wrong with me, I began to sew
plastic stars to the back of my eyelids
and my rib cage held on to kind words
inside its handsome parentheticals.
My nails grew long enough
to collect strange filaments
of soil. More than once, I folded
my heart like an old bandana
and each time it unfolded
with new questions. More than once,
I swam through my own blue rooms
without kicking up sand.

WHEN MY LAST BOYFRIEND WRAPPED HIS TRUCK AROUND A TREE

like some jagged ribbon,
all wrong and fraying in knots—
he climbed out, got checked,
then called. Stayed calm until
he said *I could have killed someone.*
When we hung up I could only
think *What are the chances I lose*
two boyfriends to something
so crude as a truck? Then, I thought
Fairly likely. This time, it was a palm
tree rather than an oak. He fell asleep
and woke up to the groaning pops
and clicks of broken steel. This time,
it was a honeyed Arizona afternoon. The bruise
across his chest, this time, from the seatbelt
became the most beautiful thing
about his body—an angry yellow sash.

I laid my head down
there and let his steady clock
lie to me: let it tell me
every synonym for safety.

BECOMING WITH

thud-hunger
with shipwreck
with douse and dig
                        lung-tight with breath
                                      with gasoline   without dogma

      still   with smoke and prayer and dagger-shine
milk bleach spill and salt
with citrus   without fracture   with bite

with open gate and eyewhite dreams

when you handwrite your full name inside me.

GROWING UP IS THE MOST LUXURIOUS THING I'VE EVER LET HAPPEN

Yes, I've given up on God
and those little yellow ecstasy pills
engraved with the Nike symbol.
Yes, I still hear something sinister
in the quiet moments, like I did as a child,
tying my shoelaces in the mornings after
the loud nights. These days, I've started to enjoy
the sound of my own name in different frequencies.
Which is to say, I'm handing out forgiveness
like raffle tickets, like tiny moons, like costume
jewelry, like cold water from the hose.
I'm so used to the dreams that lock
my legs in sludge that I explain to the others
No worries, I'll catch up soon. This always happens.
The ones where my mouth is full
of singing beetles. I've begun to pull them out,
one by one, with a shrug. Which is to say,
everything is fine. Still, I walk the dog
in the evening—her breath, small clouds,
and I look into the warmlit windows
of every beautiful home, their ordinary paintings
in frames over clean walls, and I want to get so small
I can crawl into their mailbox, wait
for a kind hand to bring me inside.

PAINTING MY HOUSE VANTABLACK

> *Vertically Aligned Nanotube Array BLACK (Vantablack coating)
> is the blackest material ever made.*

Our old black was not the absence
of light it was supposed to be.
The black dress in my closet hills
and folds, collects dust, holds my body
in reflecting light. Nothing like my walls, now:
gone. I started with the exterior—the open can
of paint, an entire hole. The roller's
round edges: dark matter floating in the bright
day. When I finished, I almost
couldn't find my way back inside.

This is not the house I grew up in.
That house is gone, too. The red grit
of brick, the walls yellowed
with tobacco and plaster. That hollow
wooden door my mother duct-taped
and painted purple after one kick
blew it apart.

All of it distorted. I stretch
my hand toward nothing
solid. I stand in the dark
memory like sun blindness.

Here in my room without walls, my house
cut out from the street—I unpin
my yellow hair, daring light.

ACKNOWLEDGMENTS

All my graditude to Alexandra Teague, Michael McGriff, Brian Blanchfield, Christopher Buckley, Laure-Anne Bosselaar, Teddy Macker, and Barry Spacks, for opening the door.

Thank you to my sister, my best friend, and the biggest love I've known. Love and gratitude for my aunt, Mikey, for making so many things possible and always standing in my corner. To Cindy, Patricia, Joe, and Aidan, thanks for taking such good care of me while I wrote this book. To my Rory dog, who was a very bad dog but a very good girl, rest easy.

Thank you to all the fantastic writers I met at the University of Idaho and UC Santa Barbara. I have learned so much from your talents, your friendship, and your careful notes. Writer friends are everything. To Lauren Yarnall, I'm so glad I high-fived you that day and said, "Yay! Poems!" My gratitude for: Cameron McGill, Stacy Boe-Miller, Garrett Chavis, Rob Thornton, Ryan Downam, Corey Oglesby, Kat Lewis, C Marie Fuhrman, Caitlin Hill, Caitlin Palmer, Canese Jarboe, Michael Landreth, Ash Goedker, Sarah VanGundy, Lauren Westerfield, Cameron Martin, Abigail Hansel, Kathleen Byrne, Gianna Stoddard, Molly Hamill, Mya McCann, Ellen O'Connell-Whittet, Andy Emitt, and more. I'm so lucky for this community and support.

Special thanks to Geffrey Davis, I'll carry your kind words and encouragement with me. To Sarah Kersey, Alexandria Ross, Jonathan Johnson, and everyone at Willow Springs Books, for your time, consideration, and hospitality.

My love to Tess, may you continue to heal. All my love, always, to Lester Lara. We miss you. Thank you for all you've taught me.

Many thanks to the editors of the following journals for first publishing these poems, sometimes in earlier versions:

Academy of American Poets: "Sister in Recovery"

American Journal of Poetry: "My Sister was a Fish, and Air"

Basalt: "*Thetys Vagina*"

Grist: "Pretty White Trash Ghazal," "A Bumper Sticker Tells Me What Belongs," "Sapphic for Asking my Brother about his Medications," "The Babysitter," "The Land of Ordinary Violence"

PANK: "Daddy," "Self-Portrait as the Thomas Fire with Displaced Laugh Track"

Raleigh Review: "Bones," "Elegy Stitched Together," "I Am Not Your Aunt"

Queen Mob's Tea House: "Paso Robles Sestina"

SALT: "With Midnight Down Your Throat You Try to Sing," "Growing Up is the Most Luxurious Thing I've Ever Let Happen," "Evacuation"

Willow Springs: "Duck Duck Goose," "Fish Tank"

Writers in the Attic: "All I Wanted"

ABOUT THE AUTHOR

Caitlyn Curran holds an MFA from the University of Idaho and currently lives in Portland, Oregon.

Her recent work can be found in: *The American Journal of Poetry*, *Basalt*, *Grist*, *Hubbub*, *Miramar*, *PANK*, *Raleigh Review*, *SALT*, *Queen Mob's Tea House*, *Willow Springs Magazine* and elsewhere.

She was a 2018 Centrum Fellow at the Port Townsend Writers Conference, recipient of a 2019 Academy of American Poets Prize, and runner-up in the 2021 Grist Proforma Contest.

WILLOW SPRINGS BOOKS

Willow Springs Books is a small literary press housed in Eastern Washington University's MFA program in Spokane, Washington.

Willow Springs Books Staff

Director	Jonathan Johnson
Assistant Director	Derek Annis
Managing Editor	Sarah Kersey
Assistant Managing Editor	Alexandria Ross
Poetry Editors	Gabe Meek & Rin Baatz
Fiction Editors	Kevin Yeoman & Megan Robinson
Web Editors	Sara Fleischer & Jackie Boutros
Social Media Coordinator	Liina Koivula

Interns

KP Kaszubowski, Jessica Parry, Oran Bordwell, Jennifer Krasner, Kelli Strain, Tristan Walde, Forest Brown, Joni Harris, Emily Allen, Sean Kyte, Kaci Webb, Meghan Laakso, Kyle Beam, Andrew Acuna, Rey Mccarthy, Joseph Self, Jessica Rodriguez, Brittany Jennings, Kayla Vanderhoof, Kasey Lecaire, Amanda Poteete, Claire Poshusta, Marcus Shoffner, Elena Axton, Theo Bell.

For a complete list of selections from Willow Springs Books and ordering information, visit www.willowspringsbooks.org.

ABOUT THE EMMA HOWELL
RISING POET PRIZE

The Emma Howell Rising Poet Prize was created in honor of Emma Howell, who was born in Portland, Oregon, and died in 2001, at the age of twenty. She lived in Spain and Brazil and traveled widely. She left behind a loving family, many close friends, and a single volume of poetry, *Slim Night of Recognition*.

Her father, Christopher Howell, served as the former Director of Willow Springs Books for over 20 years. He taught hundreds of interns what it meant to be a part of the publishing world and helped bring dozens of beautiful books into the world. When Chris retired from the press in the spring of 2021, we wanted to celebrate all the work he put into this press, as well as honor the memory of his daughter, who was an objectively brilliant poet the world lost too soon.

With this, we created the Emma Howell Rising Poet Prize in an effort to promote young writers (under the age of 35), in honor of Emma's memory. Over the past year, a group of 20+ graduate students put together this prize from scratch. We received incredible feedback and submission numbers, and feel excited watching this prize grow. *With Midnight Down Your Throat* is the debut collection in the Emma Howell Rising Poets series.

The titular poem, "Slim Night of Recognition," arrives as the final poem in the collection, of which the final lines read: "Too slowly / the final appreciation of sky / before it rolls over / and makes your last word / one of the stars." With the Emma Howell Rising Poet Prize, we strive to continue making Emma's last words heard, and to promote more bright, young, and brilliant voices.

Submissions for the 2023 Emma Howell Rising Poet Prize open in summer of 2022. More information is available on willowspringsbooks.org